D1242917

ethiopia

Traditions die slowly in Ethiopia. Although there are modern markets now, ancient open-air market places are still common.

Prepared by ALFRED ALLOTEY ACQUAYE

ethíopía

in pictures

VISUAL GEOGRAPHY SERIES

STERLING
PUBLISHING CO., INC.   NEW YORK

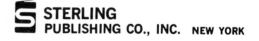
Oak Tree Press Co., Ltd.
Distributed by WARD LOCK, Ltd., London & Sydney

VISUAL GEOGRAPHY SERIES

Alaska
Argentina
Australia
Austria
Belgium and Luxembourg
Berlin—East and West
Brazil
Canada
The Caribbean (English-
 Speaking Islands)
Ceylon
Chile
Colombia
Czechoslovakia
Denmark
Ecuador
England

Ethiopia
Finland
France
French Canada
Ghana
Greece
Guatemala
Hawaii
Holland
Honduras
Hong Kong
Iceland
India
Iran
Iraq
Ireland
Israel

Italy
Jamaica
Japan
Kenya
Korea
Lebanon
Malaysia and Singapore
Mexico
Morocco
New Zealand
Norway
Pakistan
Panama and the Canal
 Zone
Peru
The Philippines
Poland

Portugal
Puerto Rico
Russia
Scotland
South Africa
Spain
Sweden
Switzerland
Tahiti and the
 French Islands of
 the Pacific
Thailand
Turkey
Venezuela
Wales
West Germany
Yugoslavia

PICTURE CREDITS

The publishers wish to thank the following for the use of the photographs in this book: Marc and Evelyne Bernheim; Church World Service; Dareus Conover; Jacques Decaux; Ethiopian Airlines; Ethiopian Embassy, London; Henri Fergen; Toge Fujihira; Alastair Matheson; Methodist Missions; Anne Pellowski; Mrs. Fred Russell; United Nations; UNICEF; United Presbyterian Church in the U.S.A.; United Press International; World Health Organization.

The smile on the face of this student at Haile Selassie University suggests confidence in the power of Ethiopia to resolve its problems.

CONTENTS

1. THE LAND 7
TOPOGRAPHY . . . RIVERS AND LAKES . . . COASTLINE AND PORTS . . . CLIMATE . . . VEGETATION
. . . WILD LIFE . . . CITIES . . . Addis Ababa . . . Asmara . . . Gondar . . . Axum

2. HISTORY 19
SOLOMON AND SHEBA . . . THE SABAEANS . . . THE AXUMITE KINGDOM . . . THE PORTUGUESE
. . . THEODORE II . . . THE ITALIANS . . . THE ITALIAN INVASION . . . HAILE SELASSIE

3. THE GOVERNMENT 26
CIVIL SERVICE . . . PARLIAMENT . . . LOCAL GOVERNMENT . . . FOREIGN RELATIONS

4. THE PEOPLE 28
RELIGION . . . LANGUAGE AND LITERATURE . . . RELIGIOUS AND FOLK DANCES . . . MUSIC . . .
Religious Music . . . EDUCATION . . . HEALTH . . . FOOD AND CLOTHING . . . ARTS AND CRAFTS

5. THE ECONOMY 52
AGRICULTURE . . . Coffee . . . Other Crops . . . Locust Control . . . Livestock . . . FISHING
. . . MINING . . . TRANSPORT AND COMMUNICATIONS . . . Roads

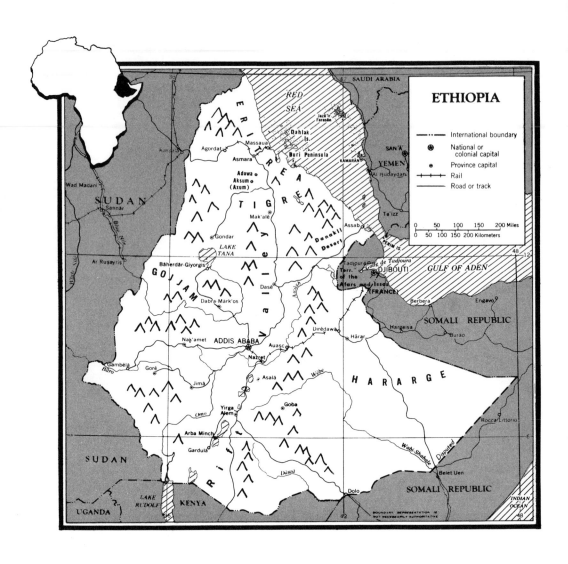

Brush and occasional trees are the typical vegetation of the drier regions of Ethiopia. This is the Awash River Valley.

I. THE LAND

A QUICK GLANCE at the map of Africa shows that the northeastern part of the continent looks like a horn. Since Ethiopia occupies that part, geographers say the country is situated in "the Horn of Africa."

With an area of 471,778 square miles, Ethiopia is somewhat larger than the combined areas of the British Isles, the Low Countries, West Germany and France; or than Texas, Oklahoma and New Mexico put together. The country is bounded on the northwest and west by the Republic of Sudan; on the south by Kenya, on the southeast and east by Somalia and on the northeast by the Red Sea and the French Territory of the Afars and Issas, formerly French Somaliland.

TOPOGRAPHY

Ethiopia is a mountainous country, with peaks more than 15,000 feet high rising from high plateaus. Ras Dashan, near Lake Tana, has the greatest elevation (15,158 feet). Of high open plains, the Amharic plateau in the central and northern part of the country and the Somali plateau in the southeast are the most extensive.

7

The Great Rift Valley splits the country from north to south. Formed by the collapse of massive blocks of the earth's surface, the Great Rift Valley is about 200 miles wide near the Red Sea coast, but as it extends to the southwest the valley narrows and breaks into long, sliver-like segments thrusting deep into the countries south of Ethiopia. The plateaus of the Rift Valley, known as *ambas*, have areas which are very fertile, and are given over to agriculture—mainly the growing of grains and the grazing of cattle.

RIVERS AND LAKES

Tributaries of the Nile and other rivers wash the Ethiopian plateaus, cutting deep gorges into the surface and often forming rapids and falls, which make transportation very difficult,

Seen here from the air, the mighty Tisisat Falls are a great tourist attraction. Described by Alan Moorehead in the "Blue Nile" as the grandest spectacle offered by either the Blue or White Nile, the waters of Lake Tana fan out over the countryside and plunge nearly 200 feet into a chasm below to form the Blue Nile.

A vast stretch of wheat covers the plateau in Arrussi province. Ethiopia could become the breadbasket of Africa, if its agricultural potential were fully developed.

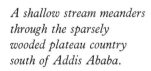

A shallow stream meanders through the sparsely wooded plateau country south of Addis Ababa.

Where road transportation is not available, vehicles are often ferried across Ethiopia's many lakes and rivers.

but provide an enormous potential for hydro-electric power.

The principal rivers are the Abbai or Blue Nile (the chief tributary of the Nile proper), the Omo, the Takazza, the Mareb, the Awash, the Wobi, and the Shebelli. The river gorges resemble the canyons of the western United States of America—their steep walls suddenly

The Koka Dam hydro-electric plant, near Addis Ababa, helps meet the country's power needs.

The port of Massawa has excellent berthing facilities. Here sacks of coffee beans await shipment.

descend from the plateaus, and as the traveller approaches them, he may find himself on the brink without realizing it. Unlike the American canyons, the walls of the Ethiopian gorges are often covered with green vegetation, which adds to the scenic effect.

The largest of the Ethiopian lakes, Lake Tana, is about 1,100 square miles in area and is the source of the Blue Nile.

COASTLINE AND PORTS

The narrow coastal plain along the Red Sea extends about 670 miles from the Sudan border to the frontier with the Territory of the Afars and Issas, near the Red Sea entrance to the Strait of Bab-el-Mandeb, the narrow passage between Arabia and Africa connecting that sea with the Indian Ocean. For the most part, the coast is semi-arid, with occasional fertile areas. The cities of Massawa in the north, and Assab in the south, near the Strait of Bab-el-Mandeb, are the only ports of any consequence.

Irrigation techniques have been introduced by the Awash Valley Authority, an agency charged with developing Ethiopia's farm output on a vast scale.

A modern bridge spans a gorge in the rugged terrain of south-central Ethiopia.

Near Assab is a desolate region of extinct volcanoes and broken lava fields, which has been described as one of the most inhospitable on earth. Off this austere and uninviting coast, are a number of small islands, of which the Dahlak Archipelago constitutes the most important group.

CLIMATE

Its high altitude gives much of Ethiopia a bracing healthful climate—the country is within the torrid zone, but the temperature sometimes reaches freezing point at the highest elevations.

The average daytime temperature, however, is between 60 and 80 degrees, with very cool nights. Thus if a visitor from New York or London were to travel to Ethiopia, he would need spring and autumn clothing. The climate of the plateaus has been likened to that of Mexico, stimulating and healthy.

Rainfall in Ethiopia is rarely torrential and the air is generally dry. There is a short rainy

These students are working in a nursery near Addis Ababa, where eucalyptus trees are raised. The eucalyptus thrives in areas where other trees fail, and is well suited to Ethiopia's high plateaus.

At Dire Dawa, cactus plants are scattered among a crop of sisal, whose sword-like leaves are an important source of raw material for making rope. Beyond is a coffee plantation.

season between mid-February and April, but the heaviest rains fall from mid-June to September, with thunderstorms occurring frequently. There is, however, half a day of sunshine each day of the rainy season. In the eastern region adjoining Somalia and along the Red Sea coast, the climate is hot and dry and semi-desert conditions prevail; at some low-lying points on the western border, the weather is normally hot, humid, and malarial.

VEGETATION

The importance of reforestation in Ethiopia is fully recognized by the government, which is making efforts to preserve and extend forest areas. Clearing of the land over many centuries has turned a large part of the country into semi-desert. However, in the valleys, vegetation is dense and tropical, and in most of the highlands, bushes and trees are found scattered around the small villages or hamlets. In the southern highlands the hills are covered with dense forests of evergreen trees. In and about Addis Ababa and other cities grows eucalyptus, a tree imported from Australia.

Lobelias, known in temperate gardens as dainty low-growing herbs, grow nearly to tree-size in the high valleys. In the forested areas, clematis, jasmine, roses, St. John's wort and wild relatives of the raspberry grow beneath the trees. Sycamores, laurels, myrrh and pines are also found, along with the kosso tree, whose red flowers are used in medicine as a de-worming agent. In the arid regions a common plant is sansevieria, popular in England and America as a houseplant, where it is often called snakeplant and bow-string hemp.

13

Coffee, which is a major plantation crop of Ethiopia, is also found growing wild in the Kaffa district, and is believed to derive its name from that area—although most dictionaries give the word an Arabic origin.

WILD LIFE

Ethiopia boasts of a variety of wild life, and many parts of the country attract foreign hunters and tourists for this reason.

Most of the familiar African mammals are to be found—elephants, zebras, giraffes, lions, leopards, antelopes, rhinoceroses, hyenas and baboons. Hippopotamuses and crocodiles are found in lakes and rivers, and reptiles and fish abound. In the Great Rift Valleys beautiful species of game fowl abound, as well as cuckoos, weaver birds, hawks, eagles, pink flamingos and flycatchers.

An animal of considerable value as far as the economy goes is the civet, a cat-like mammal with long dark grey hair and spots and bands on its back. The civet possesses glands near its tail where a musky substance is secreted, similar to that of the skunk and polecat. This substance, called civet, is unpleasant in itself, but is highly prized as an ingredient in perfume manufacture, for it serves as a fixative, that is, it captures and holds the delicate fragrance of flower extracts. Ethiopia is the world's chief supplier of this product.

NATURAL RESOURCES

The mineral resources of Ethiopia have not been properly surveyed. So far gold and, to a lesser extent, platinum are the only metals of economic value to be mined. Surveys made during the Italian occupation indicated the presence of copper, lead, magnesium and iron. Deposits of clay and limestone are common, but they support only a modest amount of brick and cement manufacture so far. There are also extensive salt deposits. Recent surveys indicate petroleum deposits on the Red Sea coast and potash in the Danakil region.

CITIES

Most Ethiopians live in small villages and there are few large towns.

ADDIS ABABA

Addis Ababa is the capital of Ethiopia and the headquarters of the United Nations Economic Commission for Africa. It is also the

Crocodiles are numerous in Ethiopia's lakes and rivers. This specimen was shot in the Awash River.

A farmer guides his patient donkey against a background of new buildings and busy traffic in Addis Ababa.

This imposing building is Africa Hall in Addis Ababa. A gift from the Ethiopian Government to the United Nations, Africa Hall is the headquarters of the United Nations Economic Commission for Africa and a meeting place of international conferences.

The Ethiopian Royal Band marches past a building under construction, at a busy intersection in Addis Ababa.

seat of the Secretariat of the Organization of African Unity.

Visitors to Addis Ababa will be interested to see Africa Hall, where many international conferences have taken place. In 1963, it played host to the historic summit meeting of African heads of state from which emerged the Charter of African Unity.

Situated on the Amhara plateau in the heart of Shoa Province, Addis Ababa has a population of more than 500,000. The city is 8,200 feet above sea level, which gives it a springlike climate throughout the year. Although Addis Ababa became the capital of Ethiopia in 1896, its real development began with the completion in 1918 of the railway connecting the city with the port of Djibouti in French Somaliland.

ASMARA

After Addis Ababa, the largest town is Asmara, with 130,000 people. This city served as the capital of Eritrea when that area was under Italian rule. Set amid rich farmlands at an altitude of over 7,000 feet, Asmara is a handsome city, with many impressive public buildings.

GONDAR

From Addis Ababa, one can easily visit Gondar, which was the capital of Ethiopia from the 16th to the 18th centuries. Gondar, about 20 miles to the north of Lake Tana, is one of the most interesting cities in the country, and remains a major tourist attraction because of its wealth of architectural wonders. During the reigns of Emperor Fasilidas and his successors, many castles, palaces and fortifications were built. The architectural details of these structures are strongly reminiscent of medieval Europe. This similarity is due to the influence of the Portuguese, who were the first Westerners to establish contact with Ethiopia. Greek craftsmen helped in the interior designing of some of the later buildings.

Not only are there many castles in Gondar, but the city was once famous for its many beautiful churches, most of which were destroyed in 1887 by invading Moslem fanatics.

Of those remaining, Debre Berhan Selassie, erected by Emperor Iyasu the Great between 1682 and 1706, attracts many tourists and pilgrims. Built on a hill in the northern part of the city, Berhan Selassie is rectangular in shape. On the walls and ceilings of the church are fresco paintings of angels, saints and devils. On entering the church, you will be met by a priest who will politely ask you to remove your shoes. This custom, considered a sign of respect in all Ethiopian churches, is also observed in Moslem houses of worship.

AXUM

The journey from Gondar to Axum can be by bus. Axum was an imperial city in the early Christian era. What still makes Axum noteworthy is the number of beautiful tombs found in the city. Among these tombs are giant steles, upright stone slabs, which served not only as the abodes of the spirits of the deceased, but were also the landmarks of the tombs of the ancient kings. It was believed that the steles represented the gateway through which the soul of the deceased ascended to the celestial sphere.

In this pool in Addis Ababa, the baptism of Christ is celebrated every January. A special ceremony is held in which the Emperor presides over the re-enactment of his own baptism.

Standing before the Cathedral of St. Mary of Zion in Axum, these Ethiopian priests wear the native dress, or shamma.

Southwest of the steles are the thrones of kings and bishops, where until the Middle Ages coronation ceremonies took place. In the southeast part of the city stands the holiest sanctuary in all of Ethiopia, the church of St. Mary of Zion. It is said that the Tablets of the Holy Ark of the Convenant rest in the church's "Holy of Holies." In the interior of the church are wall paintings showing important events in Ethiopia's religious history. There is a treasury on the left of the church which houses an impressive collection of gold and silver crosses, manuscripts, paintings and crowns of Emperor Menelik II (1889-1911).

To the northeast of the standing steles is the Mai Shum Reservoir, widely believed to have been the Bath of the Queen of Sheba. The visitor can also see two tombs which house the remains of Emperor Kaleb (514-542 A.D.) and his son Gabre-Maskal, which according to tradition once contained great riches in gold and pearls.

A visit to the city of Axum will be incomplete without seeing the church of Abba Pantaleon, founded in the 6th century by one of the early saints of the Ethiopian Church, who came on a pilgrimage from Syria to settle at the present site.

This rich collection of ancient crowns and imperial vestments worn by Ethiopian rulers centuries ago is exhibited in the new cathedral in Axum. Formerly they were in the 300-year-old Cathedral of St. Mary of Zion, where the emperors of Ethiopia were formerly crowned.

2. HISTORY

ETHIOPIA, FORMERLY CALLED Abyssinia, has a rich and ancient past. Long before the birth of Christ, when Rome and Athens were beginning to emerge as great nations, civilization already existed in the highlands of eastern Africa. In the Book of Job in the Old Testament of the Bible, for instance, one reads concerning the the wealth of the country: "For the price of wisdom is above rubies, the topaz of Ethiopia shall not equal it, neither shall it be valued with pure gold." In the 5th century B.C., the Greek historian Herodotus referred to the people of Ethiopia as "a blameless race," "a high-souled folk," and "the most just men."

SOLOMON AND SHEBA

Ethiopians claim that they spring from the Queen of Sheba's union with King Solomon of Jerusalem—this is the story of Ethiopia's royal genealogy as handed down through many generations. In 980 B.C., Makeda, the Queen of Sheba, ruled from Axum, where she worshipped the sun, according to the legend. Hearing about

the wisdom of King Solomon of Jerusalem, she decided to lead an expedition to the court of the King. When at last the Queen reached the court of Solomon, she learned much from the King. In time she was ready to go back to her country to put into practice what she had learned. King Solomon, however, had been attracted by the beauty of Queen Makeda, and wished her to be his.

The legend relates how the King resorted to a trick to gain her consent. A feast was prepared for Makeda and Solomon ordered his servants to put plenty of spices into the food of the Queen so that she would later become thirsty. At the end of the feast, the King made the Queen promise that she would take nothing from his palace. During the night, the Queen became thirsty and drank from a cup of water which King Solomon had deliberately placed in the room. Solomon, who was spying on her, caught her drinking from the cup and accused her of violating their agreement. The Queen, therefore, consented to their union. They had a child and named him Ebna Hakim meaning the "son of the wise." When Ebna grew up he ascended the throne of his mother as Menelik I, thus establishing the Solomonic dynasty of Ethiopian emperors.

THE SABAEANS

Ethiopia figured in Greek myth—Memnon, King of Ethiopia, whose mother was Eos, Greek goddess of the dawn, fought on the side of Troy against the Greeks. However, it is not clear whether the Ethiopia of the Greeks corresponded exactly to modern Ethiopia; many scholars hold that the classical Ethiopia lay far up the Nile, just short of the present country of the same name, in what is now the Republic of Sudan.

The known history of Ethiopia starts with the Sabaean immigrants from southern Arabia (Saba is another form of Sheba), who crossed the Red Sea sometime between 2000 and 1000 B.C. These people spoke languages of the Semitic group—a group which today is represented by Arabic, Hebrew and the Ethiopian languages, Amharic, Tigré and Tigrina.

The first immigrants settled along the coast. As time went on they went inland into the highlands of Tigré and Eritrea and during the 1st century B.C. established their capital, Axum, which became a hub of learning and political power.

THE AXUMITE KINGDOM

Archaeologists trace the history and culture of present-day Ethiopia from the Axumite Kingdom. Through Adulis, the port of Axum (near modern Massawa) Egyptian sailors, Syrian and Indian merchants traded in Nubian gold, copper, Roman olive oil, utensils and iron spears from the East. Axum also conducted a brisk trade in ivory and rhinoceros horn. Although few authenticated records have come down to us, it is known that the city became powerful militarily and commercially over the period 1-500 A.D. One important development of this period was the introduction of Christianity in the 4th century by St. Frumentius, who was consecrated first bishop of Axum in 326.

Hidden in almost impenetrable mountains, Medhane Alem is one of 11 mysterious solid-rock churches of Lalibela in northern Ethiopia. These churches were carved entirely by hand and their architecture is believed by some to date as far back as the Axumite period.

The wealth of Axum was so impressive that in the 6th century an ambassador of Byzantine Emperor Justinian on reaching the court of King Kaleb of Axum to negotiate a commercial treaty, was moved to describe the King as follows:

"The King had covered himself with a linen embroidered with gold; with a golden collar around his neck, Kaleb stood on a four-wheeled chariot, drawn by four elephants. The chariot was also dressed in gold. In the hands of the King were a gilded shield and two spears. King Kaleb was encircled by his royal council and attendants playing flutes."

The area ruled by Axum not only included part of southern Arabia, but the Axumite kings carried their campaigns deep into the lands of the upper Nile. During this period the classic Ethiopian language, Geez, developed, the forerunner of the modern tongues. Although no longer spoken, Geez is still used in the services of the Ethiopian Church, just as Latin is used in the Roman Catholic Church.

By the 8th century the Kingdom of Axum had lost its territories in southern Arabia. Arab armies conquered Palestine and Egypt, ending the long contact between those once Christian countries and Ethiopia, which was then cut off by 1,000 miles of Moslem territory from the rest of the Christian world.

In 702, Moslems attacked and captured Axumite ports, destroying Adulis. In 715, the Moslem Caliph declared that the Axumite King had become his subject. But, in fact, the

21

Moslem invasion had very little religious effect on Ethiopia, which remained a Christian state, maintaining its national traditions and clinging to the legend of the foundation of its royal dynasty by Solomon and the Queen of Sheba.

In the 12th century, following a period of foreign rule which had overthrown the Solomonic dynasty, Christian rule was restored by the Zagué line under King Lalibela. The Zagué dynasty was replaced by the Solomonic dynasty again in 1270. Between 1314-1344 King Amda Sion extended the Ethiopian Empire, conquering many Moslem territories. Under King Zara Yaqub (1434-68) there were many religious and administrative reforms. This king is also remembered for his books on religion and history.

THE PORTUGUESE

After the isolation of Ethiopia from the rest of the Christian world, the legend of a lost Christian kingdom in the East persisted in Europe. By the 16th century the daring mariners of Portugal had sailed round the Cape of Good Hope and opened the sea lanes to the Orient. One of their missions was to find the lost kingdom. Pero de Covilham, sent by King John II of Portugal, at length reached Ethiopia, where he was welcomed. He returned to Lisbon with a request from the Ethiopians for Portuguese assistance against the Moslems.

Shortly after contact with Portugal was established, Ethiopia suffered one of the worst Moslem invasions in its history, in the reign of Lebna Dengel (1508-40). The invaders destroyed most of the country's cultural heritage—important books were burnt, churches razed and many manuscripts disappeared.

When Lebna Dengel's son Claudius ascended the throne in 1540, the country was restored to its cultural dignity. In 1541, helped by the Portuguese, the people of Ethiopia overthrew the invaders at Massawa, and by 1543 the Moslem threat was removed.

The history of Ethiopia then shifted from isolation to a period of participation in the world scene from this time on. However, relations with Portugal were marred by the activities of missionaries seeking to convert the people from the native church to Roman Catholicism. By 1633, the missionaries had been expelled and Ethiopia maintained a more distant relationship with the Europeans for the next hundred years or more.

The name Abyssinia, long used by Europeans to denote Ethiopia, dates from the Portuguese period and is a corruption of Habashat, an area near the Red Sea coast.

THEODORE II (1855-68)

Until the 19th century contact with Europe was limited to the visits of occasional explorers and traders. In 1805, however, the British established a diplomatic mission in Ethiopia. The country had fallen, in the meantime, into a state of permanent civil war, with local noblemen vying with one another for power, and no permanent central authority. One of these warlords, Lij Kassa, succeeded in establishing his sway over most of the country, and was crowned emperor in 1855, taking the name Theodore II. The murder, by rebels, of two of Theodore's English advisors and Theodore's imprisonment of other British subjects, led to the dispatch of a British expeditionary force in 1868. Rebels joined the British, Theodore was defeated and took his own life. Disorder prevailed until 1872, when the ruler of Tigré province established himself as Emperor Johannes IV.

When Johannes IV died in a battle with the Dervishes (fanatical Moslem tribesmen living in what is now Sudan) in 1889, Menelik II took over the reins of government from 1889-1913. The history of modern Ethiopia begins with

the reign of this monarch. Through his foresight and energy, Ethiopia became a unified country and today he is considered to be the greatest of the modern emperors of Ethiopia.

During the reign of Menelik, Ethiopia became the object of Italian colonialism. Italy, itself only recently unified at the time, joined the other European powers in the scramble for territory in Africa in the late 19th century, gaining a foothold in Eritrea in 1870. From this time on, conflict with Ethiopia was inevitable.

THE ITALIANS

The story of the Italians begins with the treaty of Uccialli, negotiated for Italy by Count Antonelli in 1890. Two copies of the treaty were prepared, one in the Ethiopian language,

In Gondar, one can see romantic castles built in Portuguese style in the 16th century.

Ancient Ethiopian spears, shields and harps were displayed in the Ethiopian exhibit at the World Trade Fair in the New York Coliseum. The shield shown here is made of hippopotamus hide, richly ornamented.

place and the Italian Army of about 15,000 was defeated. Italy later negotiated a treaty recognizing Ethiopia's independence.

Upon Menelik's death, his grandson Lij Yasu succeeded to the throne. He was deposed in 1916, and Menelik's daughter, Zauditu, became Empress, and Ras Tafari Makonnen, a grand-nephew of Menelik, was proclaimed her heir and successor. The Empress died in 1930 and on November 2nd of that year Ras Tafari Makonnen was crowned Emperor under the name of Haile Selassie.

THE ITALIAN INVASION

The Italians invaded Ethiopia once again in 1935. They had previously (beginning in 1889) occupied the greater part of the Somali coast, and had retained control of Eritrea. The boundary between their colonies and Ethiopia was in dispute. In 1934, shots were exchanged across the border and the Italians, after mediation attempts broke down, entered Ethiopia. They completed their conquest in 1936. Haile Selassie took refuge in England, and the Italians remained in control of the country until World War II, when Haile Selassie, with British and Ethiopian troops, re-entered it and overthrew the Italian forces in 1941.

Since that time Ethiopia has followed a generally peaceful existence. There have been occasional minor disturbances—an attempted coup d'état in 1960, unrest among the Afar tribesmen of southern Eritrea in 1968, tension with Somalia over Ethiopia's boundary line with that country—but in the main, the country has been free to develop itself, and to combat the serious problems of illiteracy, disease, drought, erosion, and under-development of industry.

HAILE SELASSIE

His Imperial Majesty Haile Selassie I is the 225th active successor of the Solomonic dynasty. The name Haile Selassie means "the power of the trinity" and his official titles also include "Elect of God," "King of Kings" and "The Lion of the Tribe of Judah."

Amharic, and the other in Italian. On the strength of the Italian treaty, the Prime Minister of Italy, Crispi, made it known to all European countries that Ethiopia had been made a protectorate of Italy. European countries therefore began to adjust their maps accordingly.

Menelik II on discovering this, protested immediately that the wording of the treaty in Amharic gave him the right to ask for help from Italy in times of need, but that the purpose of the treaty was not to make Ethiopia a territory of Italy. Menelik II at once wrote to Queen Victoria, the German Kaiser and the President of France, insisting that Ethiopia was still a sovereign and independent nation. In 1893, he denounced the treaty and by 1895 Ethiopia and Italy were at war.

When the Italians declared war on Ethiopia, Menelik II had already prepared his forces for battle. In March, 1896, the Battle of Aduwa took

Emperor Haile Selassie, seen here in his ceremonial dress, has ruled longer than any other world figure.

Haile Selassie I was born at Ejersa Goro on July 23, 1892. His father was Ras Makonnen, who fought with distinction in the famous battle of Aduwa in 1896. Menelik II was impressed by the intelligence of Haile Selassie, and although he was only 14 years old, the Emperor appointed him a governor and granted him the title Dejazt Match, one of the highest ranks in Ethiopia.

Haile Selassie is greatly revered by the Ethiopian people, for it was he who decreed the nation's first written constitution seven months after his ascension to the throne on November 2, 1930. Through his efforts, Ethiopia became a member of the League of Nations in 1923. Since then he has done much to improve the standard of living of the people.

His appeal to the League of Nations for help in 1935 still lingers in the minds of historians:

"Should it happen that a strong Government find it may with impunity destroy a weak people, then the hour strikes for that weak people to appeal to the League of Nations to give its judgments; in all freedom God and history will remember your judgment."

His title "The Lion of the Tribe of Judah" has a living symbol: in his palace can be found a pet lion.

The Parliament Building in Addis Ababa is quite properly adorned with lions, since the lion is the symbol of Ethiopia, and appears on the national flag.

3. THE GOVERNMENT

THE GOVERNMENT OF ETHIOPIA is a constitutional manarchy with the Emperor as head of state. Under the constitution of 1930, Ethiopians were for the first time entrusted with executive and administrative powers to help the sovereign in running the country's affairs. The most important aspect of the 1930 constitution was the supremacy given to the cabinet, and the relative weakness of the parliament, whose members were appointed by the emperor, and not elected by the people.

However, it became clear after World War II that the people were ready to assume more of the responsibilities of government. In 1955, therefore, the Emperor revised the constitution. This time more democratic liberties were given to parliament, and adult suffrage and right of election to the lower house of parliament were conferred on both men and women.

Succession to the throne, the powers of the Emperor, the ministers, the judicial system and the duties of the people were spelled out.

The revised constitution has 29 articles dealing with civil liberties—the old constitution had only 11. Freedom of the press, speech, and assembly were assured by the 1955 constitution.

In 1966, in a radio broadcast, the Emperor announced further changes in the constitution. In accordance with Article 27 of the constitution, which empowers the Emperor to make changes in the government, the Emperor delegated to the Prime Minister, who is himself appointed by the Emperor, the power to appoint cabinet ministers.

CIVIL SERVICE

Under the present administration, a civil service commission has been set up for the purpose of recruiting qualified personnel for posts up to the rank of assistant minister. There is also an insurance plan for sickness and disability. Since its introduction the civil service commission has reorganized public administration in the country.

PARLIAMENT

The parliament of Ethiopia has two chambers, the Senate and Chamber of Deputies or lower house. To be elected to the lower house the candidate must be Ethiopian-born, of an age above 25, and elected through adult suffrage. Apart from the requirement that he be a bona fide resident of the electoral district, the candidate must be of sound mind and must have not committed crime. He must own immovable property valued at $2,000 or more. The number of deputies is determined according to the population.

Members of the Senate are appointed by the Emperor for a period of six years. The number of Senators is not to exceed one-half of the total number of Deputies. A Senator must be a prince or a former high government official.

A Senator must not be less than 35 years of age and must be an Ethiopian by birth. The sovereign appoints the president and two vice-presidents of the senate. When parliament is not in session, the Emperor may proclaim laws as decrees, in accordance with the constitution. Such decrees are, however, presented before parliament, when it convenes, for approval or amendment. In most instances, parliament has amended such decrees. Parliament is given the right to initiate laws.

LOCAL GOVERNMENT

A Governor General is appointed by the Emperor to be in charge of each of the 14 provinces of the empire, as a means of stimulating local development. One of the present provinces, Eritrea, had been an Italian colony before World War II, and was federated with Ethiopia in 1952 by the United Nations. In 1962, however, the Eritrean National Assembly dissolved the federation and voted for full union with Ethiopia.

FOREIGN RELATIONS

Ethiopia's foreign policy is that of non-alignment, and is aimed towards the maintenance of peace and freedom in the world. A founding member of the United Nations, Ethiopia has long maintained that the United Nations is the best means for the maintenance of peace and security in the world.

In view of Ethiopia's strong participation in the activities of the United Nations, the country was chosen a member of the 18-nation Disarmament Committee of that organization. Ethiopia participated in the peace-keeping operations in the Congo, in the Suez crisis of 1956, and in the Korean War. Presently the headquarters of the United Nations Economic Commission for Africa are maintained in Addis Ababa. In Africa also the country has been in the forefront in promoting for African Unity.

In 1963 the country played host to the first Summit Conference of the Heads of State and Government of Independent African States.

Amharic tribesmen and their children often have names which are as cheerful as their faces. Boys may be called Hagos (joy), Desta (pleasure), Mebrahtu (light) or Tesfaye (my hope).

4. THE PEOPLE

ETHIOPIA, LIKE MANY OTHER NATIONS, contains several distinct ethnic and linguistic groups. Many of the 23,000,000 people, are brown-skinned representatives of the basic physical type found in Europe, North Africa and Western Asia. Many more show admixture with the Negro race, and in some areas pure Negroes are found.

The dominant ethnic group is the Amhara, who occupy the central plateau. Closely akin to them are the Tigré people of northern Eritrea, and the Tigrina group of Tigré Province. These three groups constitute the ruling race of Ethiopia, and their languages are all Semitic, Amharic being the only official language.

Next in importance are the Galla, who are Hamitic in speech and are most numerous in the south-central parts of the country, where they live the life of nomadic herdsmen. Those living in the northern part of their range are

For a special celebration, these girls have put on the national costume.

The Danakil Desert in northeastern Ethiopia is peopled by Afar tribesmen, such as these men of Wollo Province.

Young women and children of Harar pause for refreshment, some carrying baskets on their heads.

With an umbrella over their heads and crosses in hand, priests wait outside a church. The priest second from the left also carries a censer, which contains incense.

Church attendance in Ethiopia is impressive. These church members and visitors congregate outside of Trinity Cathedral, Addis Ababa, one of the largest churches in the Ethiopian Empire.

Christianized; others are Moslems; but the original animist (nature worship) beliefs of this people survive to a marked degree. Other groups are the Afars of southern Eritrea, and the Somalis of the arid regions adjoining Somalia, both of Hamitic speech. The Shangalla are a large group of Negroid tribes living along the western border.

In addition, there are many thousands of Italians, who were encouraged to remain after World War II, because of the humane treatment shown them by Emperor Haile Selassie; and smaller numbers of Indian, Greek and Syrian merchants.

RELIGION

Nearly half of the people of Ethiopia are Christians, members of the Ethiopian Orthodox Church. In spite of its name, the Christian body of Ethiopia is not an Eastern Orthodox church, but belongs to the Monophysite branch of Christianity, which also includes the Coptic Church of Egypt, the Armenian Church and the Syrian Jacobite Church. The Monophysites split from the main body of Christendom in the 6th century A.D., following a disagreement over the nature of Christ's divinity. As in the Roman Catholic Church, however, veneration of the Virgin Mary is an important feature of daily worship. A very large number of Ethiopians are Moslems, especially in the lowland regions, and there are many Animists.

A curious minority are the Falashas, a tribe whose religion is a form of Judaism mixed with pagan practices. This sect is ignorant of the Talmud (the accepted body of Jewish law), knowing only the Old Testament and various other writings as the source of its beliefs in one God. Furthermore the Falashas are wholly unacquainted with Hebrew—their scriptures are all written in Geez. Although they observe Passover, the feast of Purim is unknown to them. They also are limited, by strict rules, in their contact with other people—for example, a Falasha may not enter the house of a Christian.

An impressive gate leads into the grounds of a church in Asmara. Many churches in Ethiopia have such entrances.

If he does, he must undergo a purification ritual before entering his own house again. The origin of the Falashas is a mystery—the likeliest explanation being that they are a Hamitic group akin to the Galla, who at some point long ago adopted Judaism. There seems little likelihood that they are actual descendents of the ancient Jews, although they claim descent from the 10 lost tribes of Israel. The true Jews do not accept them as co-religionists, in any case.

This young priest in a religious procession is carrying a Coptic Cross. The Ethiopian Orthodox Church is in communion with the Coptic Church of Egypt, and not with the Greek Orthodox Church.

This page from a 150-year-old prayer book well illustrates traditional Ethiopian art. The scripture is written in Geez, which has its own alphabet, derived from the ancient Himyaritic alphabet of South Arabia. The modern Ethiopian language, Amharic, employs a script based on the Geez letters.

LANGUAGE AND LITERATURE

Although some Ethiopian languages are Semitic and others Hamitic, they are all related to one another, according to language experts, for the terms Hamitic and Semitic are used simply to describe two branches of a single family of languages—the Hamito-Semitic—whose speakers occupy most of northern and eastern Africa and much of southwestern Asia.

Ethiopia possesses an extensive literature—mainly dealing with law, philosophy, religion and history—in the classical Geez language. Much of this literature is translated from Greek and Arabic texts. Although Geez developed from the original Sabaean tongue introduced from Arabia, the Axumite kingdom for a time used Greek as its official literary language and Geez did not come into its own as a literary tongue until that kingdom was already well established.

Classical Ethiopian poetry consists almost entirely of hymns, of which the most popular is *Weddase Maryam*, an ode in praise of the Virgin Mary, the date and authorship of which are uncertain.

Drama occupies a special place in Ethiopian life. It is an inborn quality of every Ethiopian to use gestures, facial expressions and dramatic dialogue to hammer home his points. These are all found in Ethiopian drama. In a country where, until recently, 90 per cent of the people were illiterate, the acting out of religious and historical events has been especially important.

Even today the drama in Ethiopia is mainly connected with religion. During a Lenten service in Axum, for instance, a deacon arrives at a church on a donkey. He is received at the gate by other deacons who sing "Hosanna" and the following day he goes on top of a hill to offer prayer in praise of the Virgin Mary. Devout pilgrims line his route, singing and praying. This is a living representation of a church ceremony and the audience is partaker of the ceremony, kneeling and praying. These performances recall the passion plays of medieval Europe and the early Greek drama.

In days gone by, such passion plays were held to be so sacred that the audience was not allowed to boo or applaud. As time went on the audience was allowed to express its feelings during passion plays. Authorities say that this change came about at the end of the 19th century, when Ethiopia did away with its policy of isolation.

The first Western type of drama was staged before Emperor Menelik II. A comedy based on the fables of La Fontaine, it was produced in the Amharic language. Since then drama in Ethiopia has improved, especially in lighting techniques, scenery, settings, costumes, make-up, and stage management. The foundation of the modern Ethiopian drama was laid by such dramatists as Melaku Begosew, Fitwarari Cherinet and Yefthae Negussie. In recent years H. E. Blatten Geter, Henruy W. Selassie, H. E. Ras Bitwoded Makennen, Endal Katchew

In a folk dance, a drummer sits astride the crossed poles of the men, while the women dance to the music of the begena, krar, and masenko.

and H. E. Bakumbaras Mahtener Selassie Wolde Meskel have contributed to the country's dramatic art.

Ato Tsegaye Gebre Medhin, author of *Yeshoh Aktel* has adapted classics such as Molière's *Tartuffe* and *La Médecin Malgré Lui* and Shakespeare's *Othello* in Amharic.

Ato Menghistu Lemman, a brilliant comedy writer, and Ato Tesfaye Gassesse, who has several plays to his credit, belong to a younger

Drumming plays a major rôle in Ethiopian functions. This kind of drum is played during church services in the Gelo River Valley.

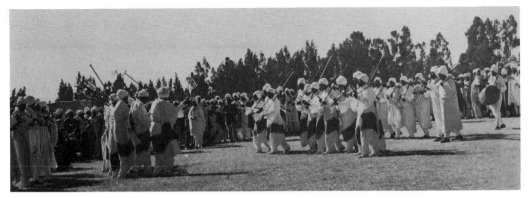

On the feast of Tim Kat (Epiphany), in Addis Ababa, Ethiopian priests perform a customary ritual dance.

generation of artists who are playing a significant rôle in Ethiopian drama. The last-named writer organized the successful performance abroad of such dramas as *Hannibal, The Queen of Sheba,* and *Love Never Dies.*

RELIGIOUS AND FOLK DANCES

Dances are usually performed on the occasion of Tim Kat (Epiphany), other festivals and holidays. Tim Kat, the celebration of the Baptism of Christ, is held usually on January 19 and is followed by the Feast of St. Michael the Archangel. On the eve of the feast all members of the churches in the area gather at a pool or a river. Arks (covered receptacles containing sacred objects) are then placed there, and surrounded by priests and cantors who sing and pray throughout the night.

At daybreak the congregation is sprinkled with holy water. Then the dance begins. The *debteras* (participants) face each other in two lines. They wear white togas and turbans, and each of them holds a staff in his hands surmounted by a cross. Drummers are nearby, ready to accompany them. The dance starts slowly. The *debteras* sing softly and follow the rhythm, swaying from side to side and at the same time raising their feet a little above the ground. The staffs are moved back and forth, up and down and the drums are beaten faster and faster. Everybody gradually becomes highly elated. When the dance is over, a feeling of nearly exhausted calm prevails.

The dance to mark the occasion of the Feast of Our Lady of Ficu or the Festival of the Palms is also interesting. On this occasion, on the Saturday or Sunday of the Festival, the choir of the *debteras* put on their long, decorated capes and togas and slowly advance, chanting, towards the church. They prostrate themselves and rise again. With palm leaves in their left hands, they cover their faces as a sign of respect. Then forming two long rows facing each other, the clergy, in their embroidered capes and snow-white turbans, dance to the cool and serene beat of the drums and *sistra*, metal rattles similar to ones used in ancient Egypt. They part, meet again and dance slowly.

The type of dance or music reflects the area where a ceremony is held. People living in the valleys and hot plains below the plateaus enjoy fast, boisterous songs and dances. In comparison those who live in the great plateau take things calmly and enjoy music and dance which reflect their restrained character.

Intricate footwork or body movements are not seen in Ethiopian folk dancing. However, there is much jumping, thumping of the feet and swaying from side to side. Movement of the body from waist to the knees is not considered healthy by Ethiopian women—the women use the head, neck and facial expressions to show their mood at the time of the dance.

Each ethnic group has its own dance and songs. The songs and dances of the Guroge in Gojjam province are graceful and sophisticated, and are very popular in Ethiopia. Most of the

35

songs of Gojjam are about love, "My heart melts for you, why don't you come" is a popular phrase in Gojjam songs. Also popular are the songs and dances of the Wollamos, who live in the south of Ethiopia, which are appreciated for their rhythmic and exciting quality. The Wollamo women dance in graceful patterns while the men make fearsome facial expressions.

Special costumes are used for all these religious and festive dances. During a religious dance, the people of Axum, for instance, instead of putting the *shannen* (scarf) around their body, wear it on their heads. This is a sign of respect and modesty.

The Somali people are warlike and this is reflected in their vigorous dances. The men wear bright towels wrapped around their legs and beautiful shirts and caps. The women wear skirts of striped cloth over a tunic and white scarves on their heads. The chief carries a dagger in hand while the men wield staves of wood. The men lower their staves as the women raise their umbrellas and vice versa to the tune of the music. The *hota*, or loyalty dance, is performed by a group of warriors. This is performed to mark an occasion, to frighten an enemy, or to express loyalty to war leaders, and is accompanied by shouting and clapping of hands or the Kabero.

MUSIC

Through Ethiopian music, one can learn the character of the people and much about their feeling for their country, for Ethiopians like to compose songs about their land, their farms, the high plateaus and the broad plains.

If you spent a night in Ethiopia you would hear melodious music—beautiful songs sung by the people, accompanied by drums, or stringed instruments, or often unaccompanied. If you listened to the singers carefully and asked for the meanings of the songs, you would be told that they were songs commemorating either a hero or loved ones or a great chief.

There are many instruments accompanying Ethiopian music. Popular stringed instruments are the *begena* (a harp), the *krar* (a lyre) and the *masenko* (a viol), with one string only, played with a bow. The *meleket* is the most popular wind instrument. A trumpet-like instrument about $3\frac{1}{2}$ feet long, the *meleket* is made of wood covered with skin. It resembles the ancient Greek trumpet and the Latin tuba. In the church, however, no instrument is used except sistrums and drums to accompany the voices.

RELIGIOUS MUSIC

The origin of Ethiopian musical chant is attributed to Saint Yared, who lived about the 6th century A.D. and who composed a large number of chants and liturgy for the church. His works referred mainly to the seasons, the months, the days and festivals of the saints and of the Holy Trinity. It was said that Yared composed chants unequalled during his time.

It is said that his works were admired in Greece, Egypt, Syria and Rome. The deeply religious nature of Yared is reflected in these words: "Allow me to retire to the forest that I may devote the rest of my life to undisturbed meditation and prayer." "Oh Music! I heard in Heaven the song of Angels!"

The new system of education in Ethiopia is providing classrooms for more and more youngsters.

All the chants of Yared and his successors were composed in Geez.

EDUCATION

Throughout Africa today, governments are making efforts to solve educational problems, and Ethiopia is no exception—nearly 20 per cent of the national budget goes into education. In the past, the church formed the nucleus of Ethiopian education. Students learned the Psalms and the Gospel in Geez. Though this kind of education had cultural and moral value, it was insufficient to meet the demands of a developing country.

Seriously concentrating on their work, these students of a mission boarding school are learning to sew.

These school boys in Dembidallo are exercising between classes.

At the Dembidallo School for the Blind, these men are learning to type in Braille.

More and more children are attending school, to take advantage of the educational facilities that the government has to offer. These children are assembled in the school yard before classes begin.

Many schools such as this one in the outskirts of Addis Ababa, are overcrowded and pupils in them must often share the same books.

These young men are boarding a plane at Addis Ababa for the United States, where they will continue their studies.

Adult education and vocational training are getting increasing emphasis in Ethiopia. This class is composed of young women learning to be telephone operators.

The idea of reforming the system of education in Ethiopia was first conceived by Emperor Menelik II, but the first full-scale effort came in the 1930's in the reign of Emperor Haile Selassie.

The first step was to increase the number of elementary schools, and to provide some vocational training to meet the industrial and agricultural needs of the country. Secondary education is devoted to the training of agricul-turalists, technicians, and forestry specialists. One big problem facing the government, however, is that there are not enough classrooms to accommodate the growing number of students. Another problem is the shortage of teachers. The government is making efforts to remedy the situation.

Ethiopia has made a strong start toward solving its educational problems. The result is that, while in the 1940's the country was able to

An Ethiopian instructor conducts a class in soil conservation in English.

These young men are studying electricity at the Imperial Communications Institute.

provide education to only about 20,000 students, in 1967 pupils in government, private and church schools totalled nearly 500,000. Of these 60,000 were in general secondary schools, and 50,000 in technical and vocational schools. At the same time there were 11,700 students studying abroad.

Other special schools are the Military Academy in Harar, the Air Force Training Centre at Debre Zeit, the Imperial Naval College at Massawa and the Haile Selassie Military School at Guennet.

Another notable achievement is that since 1967 Ethiopia has turned out teachers who are

Library services in Ethiopia are expanding. Here two students choose books from the Library of the Imperial Institute of Public Administration in Addis Ababa.

41

American Protestant missionaries are active in schools and hospitals in Ethiopia. Here a missionary and an Ethiopian minister discuss a radio broadcast.

all Ethiopian-born for the elementary schools. There were 9,000 Ethiopians teaching in the primary schools and 2,000 in the secondary schools. By 1967, all the headmasters in elementary and secondary schools were Ethiopians.

This young mother is a primary school teacher in a mission.

The most significant result of Haile Selassie's educational plan was the establishment of a university at Addis Ababa in 1961. By 1969, there were two universities and 13 colleges with a full-time attendance of 2,619. Some 2,500 more students were enrolled in the university's extension division. Recently a second university in Asmara was opened. About 1,322 students are currently enrolled in the university.

Under the present system of education, Ethiopia is turning out men and women who are helping to wipe out illiteracy in the country.

HEALTH

The Government of Ethiopia is carrying out a campaign to eradicate major diseases such as tuberculosis and malaria. Organized medical services began in 1908 with the establishment of the Department of Health. Since then Ethiopian medical services have improved greatly. In 1935, the country had only 10 hospitals and two leprosariums. It was not until 1947 that a comprehensive health plan was drawn up which aimed at providing

UNICEF has played a great role in conquering diseases in Ethiopia. In the remotest villages, vehicles donated by UNICEF carry supplies of medicine to the people.

Even though the doctor's consultation room may be under a tree, not even in a village, more and more country people are receiving medical care.

New health facilities, like the Mettu Hospital are being built in all parts of the country.

general health services, better nutrition standards and modern sanitation methods. An important feature of the plan was the training of medical and sanitary personnel. By 1967, regional health facilities were set up in 64 areas, there were 82 hospitals and a greatly increased staff of doctors, nurses and pharmacists.

Under a malaria eradication project, 1,000 workers are assigned to field operations, through which 3,248,000 people have received antimalarial protection.

The expenditure of funds for public health is now 25 times as great as it was immediately after World War II. The government has sent more and more people abroad to qualify as

Blood samples are examined under a powerful microscope in Mettu Hospital.

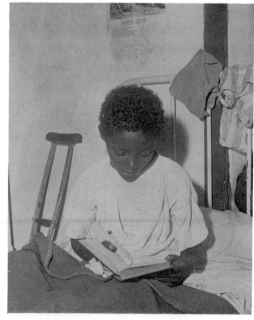

Even in sickbed, this youngster remembers to read his Bible every morning.

The combination of good health and good diet shows clearly in the face of these happy girls from the province of Hararge.

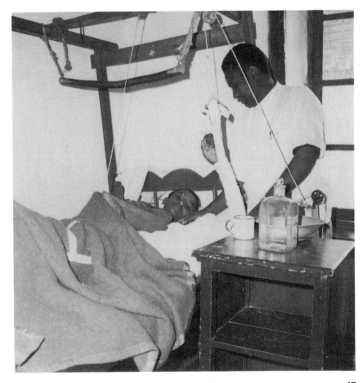

In the hospital at Dembidallo, a doctor treats a child patient, whose arm is in traction. Children as well as adults now receive proper medical attention.

A student nurse delivers a lecture on child care in a country village, using one of the local children to demonstrate her points.

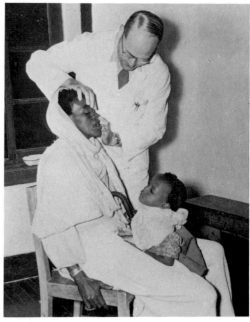

Eye infections are common in Ethiopia. Here a mission doctor examines the eyes of a patient.

These three young people are visiting nurses in a rural area. Having made their rounds in a tiny village, they are about to mount their horses and return to their clinic.

With first aid kit in hand, two nurses who have completed a two-year nursing course at Gondar College, set out on their daily visiting rounds in the town of Kolla Duba.

medical practitioners. It is hoped in time to provide one central health facility per 50,000 people and one health station for every 5,000. Ethiopia's link with the U.N.'s World Health Organization and other international agencies is helping to solve most of the country's health problems. Ethiopia was one of the first countries to sign and accept the constitution of the World Health Organization.

In the meantime, the nation's visiting nurses and medical technicians are performing a noteworthy task in bringing health facilities into the remotest villages, and in providing instruction in health care to rural mothers, many of whom are receiving such aid for the first time. The travels of these medical workers often require hard riding on muleback to reach a village stricken by typhus or relapsing fever.

These young women are being trained as community nurses and midwives to serve in rural areas.

Distribution of dried milk by UNICEF, is a common sight in Ethiopia. These mothers are lined up in a school courtyard, waiting to receive their share.

FOOD AND CLOTHING

Ethiopians drink plenty of milk, but the staple foods of the country are maize and rice. A typical dish in the Ethiopian cuisine is *watt*, which is prepared with meat, chicken and hot pepper, and is eaten with a kind of bread called *injara*. Although wheat is grown, flour is commonly made from *teff*, a grain native to Ethiopia. Ethiopia is a rich country agriculturally, but nutrition standards are poor in many areas and efforts are being made by the government to improve the diet of the Ethiopian people.

Many Ethiopians dress in the Western way, but for big occasions or for a national ceremony, they may wear the *shamma*, a flowing gown with bright-hued lining. Country people generally wear the traditional robes of their region.

In villages as well as in cities, Ethiopian nurses combat lack of good food by distributing vitamin capsules. Here a nurse examines a collection of tablets before giving them out.

The flowing shamma does not prevent this young girl from striding briskly along a street in the city of Harar.

This Ethiopian Airlines hostess is clad in the national costume, the shamma. It is made of hand-spun gauze-like cotton with a design of imperial lions woven into the border. The garment is several yards long and can be draped in many different ways, producing quite different effects.

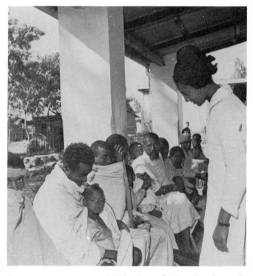

The tukul is the typical dwelling of rural Ethiopia. A circular house built of stone and baked clay with a conical thatched roof, the building has a fireplace in the middle.

A nurse reassures a child whose father has brought it for medical treatment to Kella Duba Health Centre.

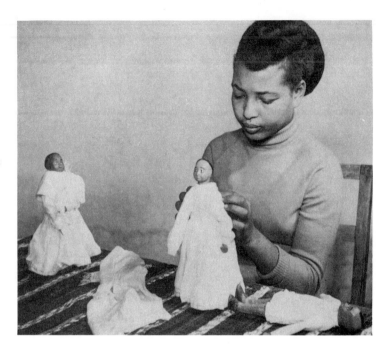

This young girl is making dolls at the Empress Menen Handicraft School in Addis Ababa.

ARTS AND CRAFTS

Ethiopia has a long tradition of religious and historical painting. Many beautifully illustrated manuscripts survive from the Middle Ages and the walls of churches and public buildings are adorned with paintings. In style these works of art show a strong resemblance to Byzantine and Romanesque painting and mosaics. A popular subject is the story of the Queen of Sheba. Other frequently seen subjects are the Virgin Mary and the saints. Modern painting is represented by Ato Asrat Wolde Medhin, who is considered one of the most talented artists in Ethiopia.

It is not only in the field of painting that the Ethiopian excels, but also in the decorative

Executed by a contemporary Ethiopian artist, Afewerk Tekle, this beautiful stained glass mural can be found in the interior of the Africa Hall in Addis Ababa.

50

Believed to be the largest market in Africa, the New Market in Addis Ababa has a variety of articles ranging from shields, spears, drums, fly whisks, and gold and silver objects to paintings of Solomon and the Queen of Sheba. Many of these articles are on display in this stall alone.

arts. Most Ethiopians, especially the women, are very skilled at making decorated household objects such as the *messob*, a decorated stand with a lid in which Ethiopian dishes are customarily served. It is a common sight to see girls and women weaving carpets by hand, and beautiful earthen pots are also made by hand.

The men are adept goldsmiths, famous for gold and silver articles used in church services. The historic city of Gondar is reputed for its fine goldsmith work.

Experts claim that Ethiopia could supply nearly 100,000,000 people with food and clothing, if the Awash River Basin were properly developed. Here Ethiopian technicians in a cable car estimate the flow of the river with the aid of a device submerged in the water and suspended from the car.

5. THE ECONOMY

LIKE MOST AFRICAN countries, Ethiopia is seeking economic and social progress through proper planning. To this end, the government launched a 5-year plan in 1957, as the beginning of a 20-year development scheme.

The plan aims to speed up the economic growth of the country, and to provide the people with good educational facilities, public health and social security. An important goal is the diversification of agriculture in order to produce raw materials for industry and commodities for export. New factories, improved transportation and modern housing are also provided for.

During harvest, farmers clean the grain by pouring it out of a small basket onto the ground. The chaff—the husk and other inedible parts—blows away, as the heavier kernels drop to the ground.

AGRICULTURE

Ethiopia lacks modern methods of farming, yet agricultural production in the country is high. Not only is the Ethiopian farmer able to produce food enough for both export and home consumption, but he is now making available sufficient raw materials to feed the growing industry of the country. For many years agriculture has remained the backbone of the country's economy—about 90 per cent of the population deriving their livelihood from it.

A British agricultural expert observes a farmer in the Danakil region plowing with a team of oxen.

Busily sorting out coffee beans, an Ethiopian girl does her part in making her country one of the leading coffee-producing nations in the world.

Although the land is rugged, the rainfall, rich soil, and varied climatic conditions make possible the production of a large variety of tropical, subtropical and temperate zone crops.

Agricultural experts state that Ethiopia has a huge agricultural potential yet to be developed. Chemical fertilizers are being put into use in the poorer areas, but modern farm machinery is

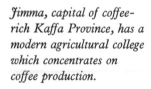

Jimma, capital of coffee-rich Kaffa Province, has a modern agricultural college which concentrates on coffee production.

Field workers tend experimental crops at an agricultural research station.

not widely used—donkeys, horses, mules, camels and oxen still provide most of the draft and field power.

COFFEE

Not many people realize that Ethiopia is the original home of coffee. Today coffee accounts for half the value of the country's exports. The coffee plantations of Ethiopia are mainly found at altitudes between 4,920 and 1,000 feet.

OTHER CROPS

Cereals—wheat, teff, barley—are important for home consumption. Other important crops are durra (sorghum), oil seeds, sugar cane, spices, garden vegetables, fruits, nuts, tobacco and cotton. Cotton is the only important crop not grown in sufficient quantity to meet domestic needs. However, a concentrated effort is being made to increase cotton output.

A United Nations expert from Israel provides technical assistance on a cotton farm.

Farmers in Ethiopia are being trained in the use of insecticides on their crops. Locusts, in particular, are a serious threat in many parts of the country.

LOCUST CONTROL

Since agriculture is the mainstay of the country's economy, efforts are made by the Ethiopian government to protect the crops against locusts, which present a serious threat.

The government has established a locust control department with headquarters in Addis Ababa. There are also locust control bases in Asmara, Dire Dawa, Dessie Makale, Gondar and Shoa, which can provide aerial spraying service to farmers.

LIVESTOCK

Livestock plays an important rôle in the economy of the country—products such as hides and skins constitute a major Ethiopian export and more than 8,000,000 sheep and goats are slaughtered annually for home consumption.

Much of the land is superbly suited to stock

These Corriedale sheep are being shipped from Nairobi to Addis Ababa for breeding purposes.

The old and the new in Ethiopia: a girl drives her flock of goats past a small aircraft parked on the Hertale Airstrip in the Awash Valley.

Animal diseases are a serious matter in a country rich in livestock. These technicians in a veterinary laboratory are examining the carcass of a goat.

Where roads are bad or non-existent, visiting nurses mount up to reach the most remote villages. Ethiopian horses and mules are small and wiry, with great endurance.

raising. Ethiopia is one of Africa's richest countries with respect to domestic animals. It is estimated that there are 25,000,000 cattle in the country, along with as many sheep, and 18,000,000 goats. Horses, camels and mules total over 7,000,000, and are valued for their strength and endurance—Ethiopian mules, in particular, are famous for their hardiness. Turkeys, ducks, and geese are raised in considerable quantities, and Ethiopia raises a large number of chickens and exports eggs to nearby countries.

FISHING

Ethiopia earns a considerable amount yearly in foreign exchange from the export of fish meal and frozen fish from the Red Sea. At Massawa there are modern processing and storage facilities for fish products, and an increasing number of people are finding employment in fishing. Surveys are being conducted on lobster fishing in the Red Sea and fresh-water sources are being studied—at Lake Tana, the Blue Nile, the Rift Valley lakes and the Awash

From a pontoon raft, engineers measure the speed of the current of a river.

River. Present government planning calls for development of the fishing industry on a large scale.

MINING

In July, 1958, a contract was signed between the Ethiopian government and a Yugoslav company for the purpose of surveying crude oil resources on the Red Sea coast of Eritrea and its adjacent islands. Their explorations confirmed the presence of petroleum in quantity, but so far it has not been exploited.

American interests have also contracted with the government for the exploration of crude oil,

At the Melka Sadi Agricultural Research Station local boys swim in the Awash River, while experts from the United Nations inspect a flock of goats.

Efforts are being made to provide more roads for the country. In the meantime, heavy-duty vehicles are widely used to drive over the open country of the plateau regions.

natural gas and associated hydrocarbons along the coastal islands and off the shore of the Red Sea, north of Massawa, and have discovered oil near Adola.

In the Danakil area, potash deposits have been found and the exploitation has started. Construction work on roads in the area, as well as on processing plants, is being carried out around the clock. Surveys also are under way to determine the presence of titanium, magnetite, chromium, graphite, nickel and iron.

The Ethiopian government is determined not to rely on foreign geologists to produce, to map out and develop the mineral resources of the country. For this reason, the Ministry of Mines has set up a Prospectors Training School. The Geology Department of the Haile Selassie University is now graduating native-born geologists.

TRANSPORT AND COMMUNICATIONS

One of the greatest strides achieved by Ethiopia has been in the field of civil aviation. Progress began in 1945, when the Ethiopian Airlines were established. Initially, the cor-

A modern bus pauses to allow a "taxi" to race past. The taxi is actually a two-wheeled cart hitched to a spirited pony.

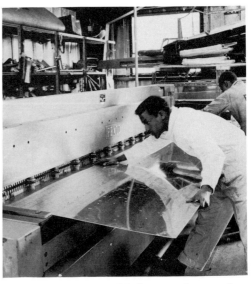

This Ethiopian co-pilot at the controls of his plane is typical of the trained personnel who operate the country's modern air service.

Shown here working with sheet metal are students of the Civil Aviation School in Addis Ababa. The School has been an important factor in improving air service in Ethiopia.

poration began with 5 Douglas C-47's. By 1956, the company had increased its fleet substantially and extended its international service as far as Frankfurt, Germany. Efficiently run and with an impressive safety record, the airline has been a major factor in Ethiopia's development.

As for shipping, the port of Massawa has the largest capacity heavy lift appliances in the

Red Sea area, and berths for all classes of vessels.

There are two major railways in Ethiopia, the Asmara-Massawa line and the Addis Ababa-Djibouti line. The latter handles the larger portion of the country's import and export trade, and serves as an important link with the outside world.

The Djibouti line, built during the reign of

In many rural areas, pumps are being set up to provide more water for the people.

Side by side with academic work, Ethiopians are also building up skills in the vocational fields. Here Ethiopian youngsters attend a carpentry class in Addis Ababa. They progress from simple carving to the making of chairs, tables and other pieces.

Radio technicians are needed to help expand Ethiopia's communications system. Many, like these men, are being trained locally.

These telephone operators were trained at the Imperial Telecommunications Institute, which also provides courses in mathematics, electricity, Morse code, mechanical drawing, business administration, and radio theory.

Modern earth-moving equipment is helping to change the face of Ethiopia. Here a tractor prepares a road bed along an irrigation canal at Ami Bara.

Menelik II, was constructed by the French Compagnie du Chemin de Fer Franco-Ethiopien. In 1946, reconstruction and modernization of the line began, and tracks and bridges destroyed during the Italian invasion were repaired. Following a treaty signed in 1959 with the French government, Ethiopia now owns half the shares in the railway.

Under the national development plan, the Ethiopian government has provided funds to expand railway services. New railway coaches and modern engines are now in service, sheds are being constructed for diesel engines and electric lights are being installed in railway stations.

ROADS

Considering the fact that Ethiopia has rugged mountains and many natural barriers, the government of Ethiopia must be commended for the progress made in providing the country with roads. Over the last 20 years, the country's road system has remarkably improved, although it is still far short of what is needed.

Ethiopia's communications system is moving slowly from the period of the pack-animal to the most advanced transportation system. Bus service to the rural areas has been greatly increased.

Until mechanization of agriculture—a major goal of the Ethiopian Government—is achieved, the camel will continue to provide transportation for farm workers in many areas.

Public health is a major concern of the Ethiopian Government. Here patients wait at a rural health station.